Antony Dufort is a painter and sculptor. Important early influences include his painter grandmother who taught him the value of drawing, the work of her own teacher, Sickert, and of his friend, Degas. *Ballet Steps* grew almost by accident out of an invitation by a young dancer to watch her in class and rehearsal. Antony Dufort was inspired by this new experience to sculpt and draw movement and dance. A systematic study of the language of ballet followed, and later formed the basis of this, his first book.

D1439389

Author photograph by Clare Park

BALLET STEPS

Practice to Performance

ANTONY DUFORT

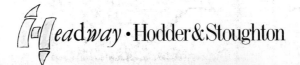
Headway · Hodder & Stoughton

Acknowledgements

Of the many people who helped me in different ways, I would especially like to thank the following: Peter Wright CBE, Director, Sadlers Wells Royal Ballet; Peter Schaufuss, Director, London Festival Ballet; Harold King, Director, and Heather Knight, Administrative Director, London City Ballet, who very kindly allowed me to attend company classes and rehearsals.

Many dancers and former dancers patiently answered my questions, even though many of these must have seemed very silly and uninformed. They explained and demonstrated steps for me time and again. They include Susan Cooper of the Royal Academy of Dancing; Marguerite Porter; Carolyn Humpston; Patricia Ruanne, répétiteur of The Paris Opera Ballet; Luke Jennings; Ric Jahn; Clare Park; and Deborah Bull of the Royal Ballet who deserves special thanks. Not only did she organise the dancers who modelled for me, but she read the proofs and offered invaluable suggestions and encouragement at every stage. The responsibility for any errors is, of course, mine alone.

I am especially grateful to the dancers represented in the illustrations: Jonathan Cope, Viviana Durante, Deborah Bull, Errol Pickford, Patrick Armand, Vincent Hantam, Carolyn Humpston, Alison Townsend, Paula Read, Karen Hutton, Jacquie, Wayne, Anita and Debbie; and also to David Coleman, Principal Guest Conductor, and the Orchestra of London Festival Ballet; David Wall CBE, Director of the Royal Academy of Dancing; and Kate Castle, former Education Officer, The Royal Ballet.

I would also like to thank Leslie Spatt and Bill Cooper who were very helpful in finding suitable performance photographs; Alex Dufort, Hugh Palmer, Jamie Muir and Richard Sparks for advice on photography and video; and finally Jesse Graham, Kate Gardiner, Sharon McGorian, Elisabetta Brodasca, Brenda Holtam, Caradoc King, Patricia White and Margot Richardson.

British Library Cataloguing in Publication Data

Dufort, Antony
Ballet Steps: Practice to Performance.
New ed
I Title
792.8

ISBN 0-340-59510-8

First Published 1990
Impression Number 10 9 8 7 6 5 4 3 2
Year 1998 1997 1996 1995 1994

© 1990 Antony Dufort

Printed in Great Britain for Hodder & Stoughton Educational, a division of Hodder Headline Plc, 338 Euston Road, London NW1 3BH by The Bath Press, Avon.

In memory of my father Timothy Dufort and my grandmother
Doris Travis (née de Halpert), a wonderful painter
who taught me everything I know,
and also Louise Abbott and Adam Sedgwick.

Contents

2: Rehearsal and Pas de Deux

Note: Words in *italics* in the text can be looked up in the Index Glossary

List of Photographs

Preface

For many people who develop a passionate interest in the ballet, being taken at the age of five or six to see THE NUTCRACKER or THE SLEEPING BEAUTY at Christmas seems to have been a turning point in their lives. I was not so lucky.

I didn't see my first ballet until I was much older. Stuck up in the 'gods' at The Royal Opera House in Covent Garden with half the stage and most of the scenery hidden from view, I couldn't see a lot, and understanding almost nothing about the dancer's art, I was not inspired by the little I did see. Some years later I had another look at the programme from that night and discovered that I had been watching Anthony Dowell and Antoinette Sibley at the height of their powers, in Sir Kenneth MacMillan's production of ROMEO AND JULIET.

Happily, in spite of my lack of appreciation a persistent friend took me to watch a company class, followed by a rehearsal. This was a revelation. Here were people I understood; real people, working with extreme dedication at the elements of their art.

In fact, I had already used dancers as models for drawings and sculpture, because they are so much more aware of how their bodies look from any angle. They are particularly good too, at holding a pose. But now, for the first time, I was looking at the fascinating variety of their shapes and movements as they exercised and rehearsed in class, and I wanted to draw and sculpt them at their work.

I found it almost impossible at first because the movements seemed to go by so quickly. I began to search for a book which would explain something of the formal language of classical ballet in a way that I would be able to understand: a book that would also explain the connections between what I saw in the classroom and the performances that I now began to watch with increasing interest on the stage.

There are many beautiful ballet books. Unfortunately they are either large and glossy, based mainly on dramatic photographs, or small and technical, full of stick-figures and outline sketches that only a professional dancer would understand. None of them seemed to capture that flow of movement which is so important to the art of dance.

Because the book I was looking for did not exist, I was forced to undertake my own research, and BALLET STEPS began.

Classical ballet is an expressive language which uses music, the human body, and the inspiration of the dancer and choreographer. Writing and illustrating BALLET STEPS has helped me to understand something of this language. I hope it will also help young dancers and their parents, and ballet-goers of all ages, to gain an understanding of the basic elements of dance and its special vocabulary. Above all, I hope it will increase enjoyment of one of the great arts of our day.

Antony Dufort

Introduction

For most of us, the image of a girl standing on *pointe* sums up perfectly what makes classical ballet so different from any other form of dance. Her shape has a mysterious quality; a flowing elegant line runs upwards from her toe, through her body, into her upraised arm and beyond. There is a feeling of balance and harmony, of effortless co-ordination. To the spectator it seems so easy, so natural, that he hardly pauses to wonder how it is done. And this is how it should be: for classical ballet is one art form for which outstanding technique is a minimum requirement. In fact, holding a position like this needs tremendous effort; and it is a tribute to the dedication and training of every professional dancer that this is the last thing we think of when watching a ballet.

It seemed natural to base BALLET STEPS on the daily class and rehearsals which make up so much of the dancer's working life, and the special training which makes ballet possible.

For me the class is fascinating. Watching dancers exercise in ordinary leotards, uncluttered by costume, makes everything clearer. So this is how I have drawn them. Slow movements and fast jumps and turns are broken down into a series of drawings across the page; and this conveys far more movement than a single dramatic photograph. The small performance photographs complete the picture, connecting practice with performance.

I took photographs first, and based my drawings on them. This way I was free to correct those tiny mistakes that spoil the classical line – a hand or a foot, even just a finger slightly out of place.

Choosing what steps to illustrate and which to leave out was very difficult. Even with a book ten times as thick as this and years more to do the drawings, I would still not have covered the full range of ballet steps. So, with the help of dancer friends and consultants, I have had to be very selective.

I had three principal aims: first of all, the steps had to be common enough for the spectator to notice in most popular classical ballets. Second, I wanted to show representative examples of all the different types of movement that the dancer is expected to master, as a soloist or in the *corps de ballet*. Third, I wanted to show what makes the *pas de deux* so exhilarating – the flow of movement and the greater range of shapes that two bodies can make when moving in harmony or counterpoint. Certain partnerships have brought an extra magic to the dance and delighted a whole generation of spectators not previously interested in the ballet.

Through their own original and creative interpretations of the great roles, dancers keep classical ballet alive, fresh and exciting. For all their rigorous training, their continual striving for perfection, ballet dancers are not robots. Sometimes, in the brilliance of a major production, dancers appear almost superhuman. They are not, of course. They are human beings as well as artists – but human beings who work, perhaps, a little harder than the rest of us. . . .

Before class begins dancers arrive loaded down with bags, and change into their practice clothes. Some of the earlier arrivals will have started gently warming up in strange positions like the ones above, called *frogs*. Because in ballet, all movements are done with the legs rotated sideways, this is a very good exercise for what the dancers call *turn-out*. Sitting or lying on the floor like this, they can gently ease the legs outwards in the hip socket. Dancers who are supple enough to sit or lie in 'frogs' without undue strain are said to be 'flat turned out', and for them it can even become a rather comfortable way of sitting! Like all dancers however, they will need to exercise constantly to maintain this turn-out while moving.

Warming up alone before class, or a performance, is such an integral part of the dancer's life that it inspired Jerome Robbins to create his own version of Nijinsky's ballet AFTERNOON OF A FAUN to Debussy's music

of the same name. On the stage, two dancers –
a man and a woman – face the audience, which
becomes for them the mirrored wall of an
empty classroom. They are so absorbed in
their own reflections that they only gradually
become aware of each other's presence. The
ballet gives us a glimpse of the dedication and
self-absorption that dancers need in order to
succeed in a very tough profession. Dancers
are of necessity young people who generally
reach their peak, physically and artistically,
by the age of 30. But though their physical
powers tend to decline, great artistry can keep
them dancing for many more years.

Retired dancers often make very good
teachers. Their great experience gives them a
special insight into the younger dancer's
individual needs, and their memory of rôles
that they have danced is very important when
ballets are revived.

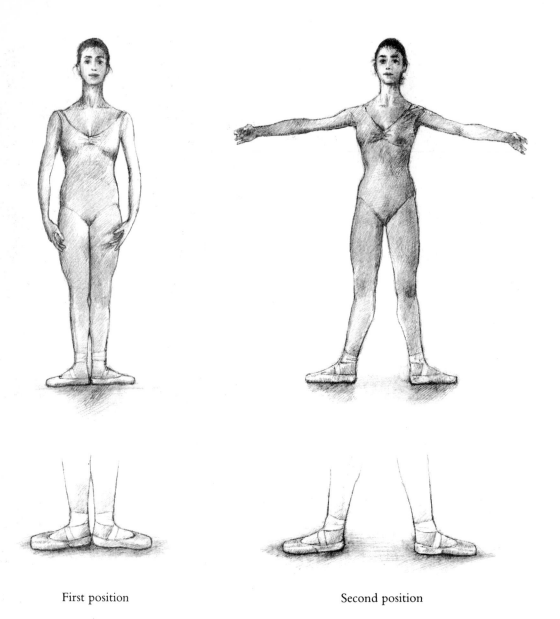

First position

Second position

The Basic Positions   Young dancers are taught the five positions of the arms and feet during their earliest lessons. Because all steps start, finish, or go through one of these positions, they form the basis of classical training. Each position allows different movements of the legs, and you should try to memorise the ones you will see most often. They are the *second position* for movements to the side, the *fourth position* for movements to the front and back, and the *fifth position* which acts as a junction for movements in all directions. There are certain qualities that all five positions have in common. The body is

Third position

Fourth position

Fifth position

perfectly poised, its weight evenly distributed over both feet; the leg muscles are 'pulled up', and the legs and feet are fully *turned out* to the side. At the same time, the upper body is relaxed and free, allowing the arms to move gracefully without any hint of strain. It is difficult for very young dancers to do the fourth and fifth positions of the feet at first, so they may do the third position instead. Professional dancers do not need to use the third position very often.

Turn-out is such a vital part of classical ballet technique, that it needs to be understood in more detail.

17

Turn-out   In these drawings we see two clear examples of good *turn-out*. In the first drawing the dancer *pliés* (bends his knees) in the *second position* while the second dancer extends his leg to the side (also in second position). The important thing to notice is that it is the entire leg, from the hip, right through to the tip of the toe that turns out, not just the foot. Also it is not just the *working leg* (the leg in the air) which turns out, but the *supporting leg* as well.

There are a lot of movements in ballet where the legs have to be lifted high in the air in different directions. Without ballet training this would be very difficult because of the design of the hip socket. Try lifting your leg high to the side and you will see what I mean. Rotating the whole leg through 90 degrees helps solve this problem, because it changes the normal relationship between the two halves of the hip joint.

Turn-out is one of the most important

ingredients of the classical line and extends the possibility of what dancers can do with their bodies. So, it has a vital effect on what we see on stage. It makes the dancers look sleek, elegant and poised, whether on the ground, or flying through the air. Turning

out also stops them tripping themselves up as they dance.

Dancers' muscles develop differently from athletes' because of their highly specialised training.

L Ballo è un'arte di muovere ordinatamente il corpo, affine di piacere agli spettatori.

'Ballet is the Art of moving the body according to certain laws of harmony, in a way pleasing to the audience.'

GIAMBATTISTA DUFORT
Trattato del Ballo Nobile   Napoli 1728

1: The Class

Introduction   Class is the daily ritual shared by all members of the company, from the most junior member of the *corps de ballet* to the most experienced soloist. It is divided into two parts, the *barre* and *centre work*. Here we see some of the wide variety of stretching exercises that dancers do before and during class.

Every dancer has his own exercises that show him which parts of the body have suffered most during the previous evening's performance, and will need most attention in class before they begin to move freely again. These exercises will also help prevent further injuries. Stretching and warming up at intervals during a long working day, the dancer can work on his own for once and concentrate his mind on the tasks ahead.

THE BARRE

Introduction   The ballet mistress and the pianist have arrived. The dancers take their places and class begins, as always, with exercises at the *barre*. In a big class, extra barres will be carried to the middle of the room to give the dancers plenty of space.

Exercises at the barre are very important because as well as warming up the muscles they are designed to increase speed and precision of footwork, to prepare for jumps and turns, and to increase flexibility and strength in the spine. They also improve balance and increase the freedom of the legs and arms to move easily in their sockets. Great emphasis is laid on developing *turn-out* and co-ordination. In the following pages we see a small sample of barre work.

A good pianist gives a cheerful atmosphere to the class and knows a hundred different pieces to suit the rhythms of all the exercises.

The very first exercise at the barre is always *pliés*. By this time, the dancers hope to be in a composed, if sleepy, frame of mind. Moving slowly up and down, occasionally checking their position in the mirror, they search for the centre of balance within their bodies which every dancer must find at the beginning of the working day.

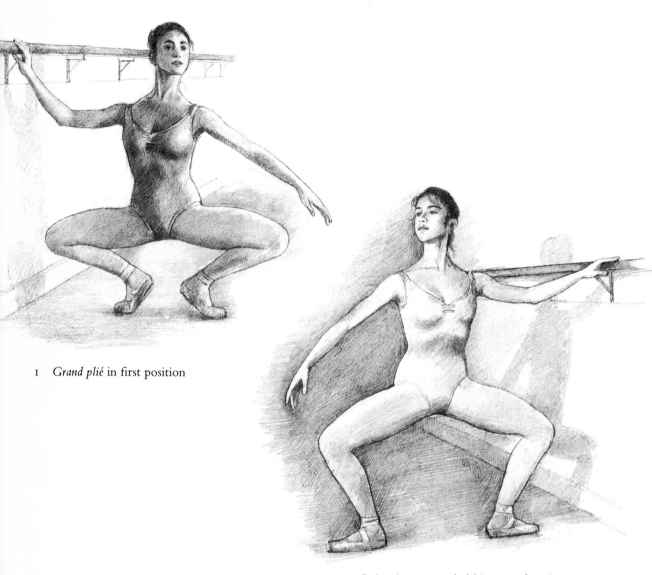

1 *Grand plié* in first position

2 Going into a *grand plié* in second position

Pliés The fluid rise and fall of *pliés* as they gently warm the leg muscles and the hip sockets is the basis of all co-ordinated balletic movement. The initial impetus and push-off for most turns or jumps comes from a plié on one or both legs. The *demi-plié* in *fifth position* [3] is used constantly in jumps where its spring-like quality is vital for take-off, and its cushioning effect for landing.

There are two types of plié: the demi-plié (half way down) and the *grand plié* (all the way down). Like other exercises at the *barre*, they are done in all five positions to practise the action of the legs to the front, back and

3   *Demi plié* in fifth position

sides. In the grand plié in *second position* where the feet are quite far apart, the tendons are not very stretched and the dancers can plié all the way down with their feet flat on the ground [see pp. 24/25, and [2] above]. In *first position* [1] and fifth position [3] where the feet are closer together, they can only go down so far

before they allow their heels to lift gently from the floor. To help them keep an absolutely straight line through the head, hips, knees and feet, and to avoid rolling on the feet and sticking the bottom out, they think of keeping the base of the spine above the heels at all stages of the plié.

1   2   3   4   5

Battements Tendus   After *pliés* come *tendus*. These consist of repeatedly extending then closing in the fully turned-out leg and foot. Tendus are done in a cross-shaped pattern (*en croix*) to the front, side and back, and are then repeated facing the other way. This helps dancers develop equal strength and suppleness on both sides of the body, so they can move with freedom and control in any direction on stage.

To get an idea of the rhythm and action of tendus, look first at just the feet. From *fifth position* [3] she tendus to the front [4] and returns; to the side [6] (see inset) and returns (this time with the tendu foot behind) then to the back [8] and returns. The exercise continues to the side [10] then closes in front to start the sequence again [9].

These apparently simple movements must be done properly if they are going to help the dancer in any way. She must be perfectly balanced, her hand resting only lightly on the

6   7   8   9   10

barre, so she could lift it at any moment. She must keep her leg fully turned-out while she extends it, so she pushes forward with her heel, stretching her foot through *demi-pointe* along the ground to its fullest extension.

As with *pliés*, the hips must be absolutely straight and square; the bottom flat, and the body *pulled up* to allow the tendu leg to return to fifth position with the knee straight. This action 'through the foot' prepares the legs for taking off and landing in jumps much later in the class.

While the legs move in this somewhat mechanical way, the arms move in one graceful and continuous movement called a *port de bras*, starting with a *preparation* [1, 2, 3].

She also moves her head, upper body and arm in harmony with the tendu leg, infusing the exercise with grace and feeling.

During performance, dancers do tendus in the wings to get their legs warmed up and 'tuned' before going on stage.

29

Rond de Jambe à Terre

The difficulty of the exercises increases as class goes on, each exercise preparing the body for the one to follow. *Glissés* will have followed *tendus*, which they resemble except that the foot slides along the ground, up into the air at the point of furthest extension. Now in *rond de jambe à terre*, the *working leg* draws a semi-circular 'D' shaped path on the ground.

The first two drawings show the *preparation*. From *fifth position* the dancer moves her left leg forward while doing a *plié* on her right leg [1]. After a pause, the leg opens out to the side, and continues round to the back [2, 3]; then comes straight forward to the front again through *first position* [4, 5] on the flat of her well *turned-out* foot. The exercise will be repeated a number of times in this direction. Then it will be reversed, moving this time towards the back and circling round towards the front. By now the body is quite hot and sweaty and ready for more strenuous exercises that require the legs to be lifted from the ground.

1 2 3 4 5

Rond de Jambe en L'Air   Here the toe traces an oval path in the air rather than on the ground. From fifth position [1] the arm and leg open out into *second position* in the air [2]. While the upper part of the leg remains absolutely rigid, the knee bends and the toe circles forward through *retiré* [3, 4], before extending back into second position again [5]. The exercise then repeats. In a double *rond de jambe* the toe makes a second small circle close to the calf muscle, and this is frequently seen on stage. In the ballets of August Bournonville for example, one often sees an upward jump from fifth position with a very quick rond de jambe while in the air. (The *rond de jambe sauté*.) With a turn of the body added (see inset) this becomes the *rond de jambe sauté en tournant*. This exercise also builds the strength and control needed for *fouettés rond de jambe en tournant* (see p. 84) which combine the rond de jambe with 32 turns and a *fondu* (bend of one leg) between each one.

Battement Fondu and Fouetté of Adage

The graceful linking of slow movements and jumps in ballet gives it its seamless romantic quality and comes from the use of *fondu*. Fondu literally means 'melted', and is really a *plié* on one leg. The fondu and the plié can be thought of, in more senses than one, as two of the mainsprings of ballet.

The *battement fondu* in the upper row of drawings shows something of the quality of movement dancers look for. She fondus with her *supporting leg* while bending her *working leg* inwards. Both legs then unfold and straighten out in one fluid and controlled movement.

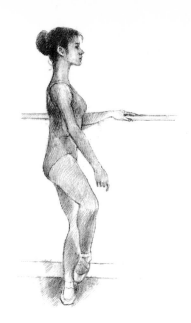

In the lower pair of drawings, the movement continues with a rotation of the body about the supporting leg. The dancer keeps her foot raised at the same height in the air, and maintains her *turn-out* at the same time. This rotation is called a *fouetté* of *adage*, which means a 'slow whipping turn'. In the *Grand Pas de Deux* from THE SLEEPING BEAUTY (p. 142) you can see a similar movement, where this whipping round of the hips is done

quickly with dramatic effect.

Look at the seven drawings again, and imagine the dancer's body slowly folding and unfolding in the fondu, and continuing in a slow and graceful rotation, ending in an *arabesque fondue*, as one continuous chain of movement. This is a small example of the language of classical *choreography*.

Développés   The *développé* is a slow,
unfolding movement of one leg. It is an
essential feature of *adage*, the kind of slow,
sustained and frequently very moving dance
seen for example in the *Grand Pas de Deux*.

On stage, you may see the ballerina
développé alone, while supported by her
partner (see inset), or during a high lift. Here
it is particularly difficult because she may be
leaning backwards and off balance, or her
partner may be carrying her across the stage.

Développés at the *barre* are exercises designed
to give the body the necessary strength and
control to raise the *working leg* to the height
of the shoulder and above, and hold it there,
without apparent effort.

The drawings show three different sorts of
développé: *devant* (to the front) [4], *à la seconde*
(to the side) [8], and *derrière* (to the back) [12].
Starting with *développé devant*, she raises her
foot from *fifth position*, through *sur le cou de
pied* (by the ankle) [1], *retiré* [2], through a
half-way position with the knee bent in front
called *attitude devant* [3], to développé devant [4].

34

Then she développés to the side. Starting from fifth position [5], through sur le cou de pied [6], retiré [7], and into *développé à la seconde* [8]. Finally, she unfolds her leg to the back (derrière), again raising her leg to retiré [9, 10], but this time, she unfolds it through *attitude derrière* [11] to *développé derrière*, also called *arabesque* [12]. Here she keeps her back as high as possible, though it is natural to tilt the pelvis slightly to raise the leg behind.

All three développés finish with the leg being lowered to the ground, with the toe still pointing. It then moves through a *tendu*, and back into fifth position.

While doing développés, dancers try to make themselves as tall as possible on the taut *supporting leg*, keeping the working leg perfectly turned out from the moment it leaves the ground to the moment it returns to fifth position. Finally, they make sure that the développé itself is smooth, fluid and seamless. Later on in the book you will see two examples of the développé in use in a *pas de deux* (pp. 142, 144).

Grands Battements   This exercise is
designed to 'loosen' the hips, the hamstrings
and the back by throwing the leg as high as
possible into the air. Like other *barre* exercises,
grands battements are done to the front, the side
and the back, and with both legs so that the
dancer can develop an equal ability on either
side of the body. Good *turn-out* is particularly
useful for high battements to the side, which

the construction of the hip socket would
otherwise make very difficult. Each grand
battement passes through one of the *tendu*
positions, which can also be seen in the
drawing. The movement is controlled
throughout; the hips kept square, with no
pitching backwards of the body. Coming
down, the leg is taut and the foot fully
stretched.

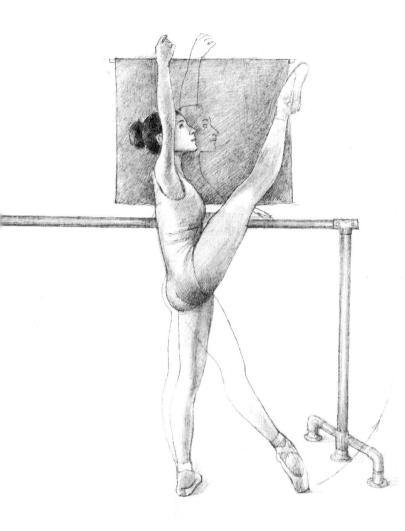

Increasingly, modern *choreographers* working in the classical style ask dancers to hold their legs in high positions. Since the same dancers also perform rôles in more traditional ballets, this has had an influence on their style in these ballets as well. Classical ballet continues to evolve, and innovations are always welcome when they do not go against the spirit of the dance. The photograph shows a modern use of a very high leg position from an American production of DON QUIXOTE, a traditional ballet.

Grands battements are impressive but actually need less strength and control than a slow unfolding *développé* ending up in the same position. There are many more barre exercises like *frappés* and *petits battements* for which unfortunately there is no space here.

CENTRE WORK

Introduction   At the end of *barre* work, there are more stretching and relaxing exercises to loosen the back and the muscles in other parts of the body that have worked hard in the previous three-quarters of an hour. If there are barres in the middle of the room, they are carried to one side. From now on all exercises will be done without their support.

Centre work can be divided into three broad sections: *adage*, which consists of slow sustained movements and *pirouettes*; *petit allegro*, which is concerned with linking steps and small jumps, and finally *grand allegro* with its big leaps and turns. Above, the company is practising a slow adage movement facing the right hand corner of the stage. When on

tour, companies frequently do their classes and rehearsals on stage because few theatres have proper studios.

Because these *centre* exercises derive from classical *choreography*, they appear similar to what we will eventually see on stage. The combinations of steps that become more difficult as the class goes on are arranged by the ballet master or mistress to stimulate and test the dancers and to prepare their bodies for the greater demands of today's choreographer. Choreography is not merely the rearranging of well-known steps. On the contrary, creating new ballets means creating new kinds of movement, which may in their turn inspire new exercises.

Effacé: open

Adage

Alignments: Introduction

Exercises in the centre often start and finish facing diagonally across the room. This is true of the later jumps and turns as well as the early slow movements done on the spot. The direction the dancers face, known as their *alignment*, is another very important element of the classical style because it controls the outline of the body that the audience sees. If all movements were done facing the front, they would become monotonous. Notice

how facing the right-hand corner of the stage, or facing the left-hand corner changes the outline of the two dancers' bodies. These different shapes show two of the most basic alignments or positions of the body. They are the open position, known as *effacé*, (or *ouvert*, meaning 'opened up') and the more compact position with the leg crossing behind or in front of the body, known as *croisé* (crossed). In either case, the hips face one corner of the stage. Standing on the other leg, but facing in

Croisé: crossed

the same direction, would change the effacé to croisé and the croisé to effacé.

Dancers must take care to use correct alignment on stage, because the beauty of the body's shape in different positions depends as much on the space we see between the limbs, as on the correctness of the position itself. If certain parts of the body are hidden, then the purity of line that the spectator sees will be lost.

To understand how alignment is

maintained you have to imagine, as dancers do before it becomes second nature, that they are standing in the middle of a square which moves around the stage with them. Invisible lines are drawn diagonally and at right angles through its centre to mark the different alignments. As long as the dancer is standing correctly within the imaginary box, keeping the front of the box parallel with the front of the stage, he will know the exact angle of his body in relation to the audience.

6

5

Effacé

4

Alignments I: Croisé to Effacé

The dancer stands on her *supporting leg* and moves her *working leg* from front to back. She goes from *croisé devant* (crossed in front) to *effacé derrière* (open, behind). These are the technical names of the positions she goes through which you can imagine being linked by a slow continuous movement from right to left. Note how the shape of the body changes as she moves. We see her as if we are sitting in the centre of the front row of the dress circle.

In the first drawing [1] she stands in croisé devant, then slowly bending her knee, she moves to *attitude croisée devant* [2], then lowers her leg to *tendu croisé devant* [3]. Slowly her leg moves back to *tendu effacé derrière* [4], also known as *arabesque à terre* (or arabesque with the toe on the ground). Then her leg moves up, bending at the knee to an *attitude effacée derrière* [5] and finally straightening out into an *arabesque* [6]. Compared to the drawings the tendu croisé devant from George Balanchine's BALLET IMPERIAL shows an exaggerated use of *alignment* in the upper body.

3

2

Croisé

I

Effacé

Croisé

Alignments 2: Effacé to Croisé

Here the dancer is aligned along the other diagonal. This time, moving the *working leg* from front to back, he goes from *effacé devant*, (open to the front) to *croisé derrière* (crossed behind). The technical names of the positions he goes through are as follows: [1] effacé devant, [2] as he bends his leg slightly inwards, *attitude effacée devant*, [3]*tendu effacé devant*. As his leg moves through *first position* to the back he extends into a *tendu croisé derrière* [4],

followed by *attitude croisée derrière* [5]. Finally he opens his leg out into an *arabesque* [6]. Now try comparing each position on these two pages with the same position on the last two. Note how different the shape of the body looks in *croisé* and *effacé* when we see the same position from the other side, and along the other diagonal. The photograph shows a tendu croisé derrière from NAPOLI, choreographed by August Bournonville.

Alignments 3: Ecarté   This is another diagonal *alignment* of the body, but it has a quite different feel from *croisé* and *effacé* because here the body is flattened on the diagonal. *Ecarté* means 'thrown wide apart' or separated, and is an extension of the *second position*, where legs and arms open out directly to the side. When a dancer is in écarté to the front as in the pictures on the left-hand page, she tilts her head towards her raised arm.

When in écarté to the back she looks down
the line of her lowered arm. Because of the
angle at which we see her, the raised leg looks
very long. This makes a dramatic shape if held
long enough for the audience to appreciate the
effect. In the two inset examples of écarté
from THE SLEEPING BEAUTY, Florestan and one
of his sisters *développé* in *écarté devant* and
Aurora is supported in *écarté derrière* by one of
her suitors.

1   Romantic

Line and Style   If you are lucky
enough to watch a ballet company rehearse
on stage you may well see two soloists practise
pas de deux from three different ballets, all in
different styles, on the same day. London
Festival Ballet for example may rehearse both
Sir Frederick Ashton's and Rudolf Nureyev's
productions of ROMEO AND JULIET at the same
time. The music is the same, but the style of
dance utterly different. Dancers take this sort
of thing in their stride!

These three drawings show the supported
arabesque in the very different shapes and
feeling of the *Romantic, Classical* and *Modern*
styles. [1] shows the soft romantic line of
GISELLE, running down the arms, back and low

arabesque leg. On stage, the Victorian
hairstyle and long dress revealing only the
ankles are both expressive of Giselle and
Albrecht's tragic story.

[2] shows a strong, clear-cut classical
arabesque. The mood in THE SLEEPING BEAUTY
is more optimistic. Aurora dances with the
prince who has fallen in love with her. The
arabesque leg is higher, the *tutu* revealing
much more of her body.

[3] shows a more gymnastic, more extreme,
modern arabesque, with the body completely
revealed in a leotard.

It is their long years of ballet training, and
a sympathetic partnership which makes these
dancers so versatile.

48

2 Classical

3 Modern

The Arabesque   In its many forms and moods the *arabesque* is seen more often than any other position of the body in ballet. We see it at its most exuberant in the *first arabesque* position on *pointe* (right), and in its male equivalent, on *demi-pointe*, above. It is used in lifts, jumps, turns, *promenades* and *pirouettes*, and in the *pas de deux*. To form an arabesque, one leg is raised and extended behind the body and a variety of shapes of the arms is used to harmonise with its long, extended line. A great artist is able to give a different emotional colour to each arabesque by subtle variations of height and carriage of the arms and legs.

The fashion for very high arabesques is quite recent. Those dancers who concentrate only

on the height of the leg at the expense of all else, risk distorting the harmony of the curve between the raised arm and the arabesque leg.

The terms *first*, *second* and *third arabesque* are used for the different arm positions that go with the raised leg. In different countries the positions themselves may vary as well as the way of naming them, but shown here and on the following pages are those most commonly used.

The extra few inches that going on *pointe* gives a girl means that her partner must be taller than her. Sadly this can sometimes hold back the career of a tall girl in certain companies.

First Arabesque In the photograph above, from the famous Rose Adagio in THE SLEEPING BEAUTY, Aurora steps out on to *pointe*, alone, poised and regal, in *first arabesque*. Her three suitors who have *promenaded* her in turn, watch admiringly in the background.

It is very important in the arabesque to keep the hips as square as possible, and facing the front, and to avoid the natural tendency of the arabesque leg to pull the hip upwards. At the same time, *turn-out* must be maintained, so the arabesque leg in both the drawing and

the photograph is rotated in the hip socket, causing the heel to turn away from us.

Very often you will see a dancer standing in first arabesque rotating slowly on the flat of the foot. She does this by making a succession of tiny movements with her heel.

They must be done very smoothly to avoid any up and down movement of the arm or leg. Done in this position it would be called a *promenade* in first arabesque.

Second Arabesque   The position of the arms seen in the *first arabesque* has been reversed. The arm nearest us now points forward, extending the long line of the leg on the same side of the body, instead of being held above it and parallel as before. The crossed line of the arms causes the dancer's upper back to turn very slightly towards us, revealing the shoulders, and adds a feeling of yearning, of physical and emotional tension. Later on (p. 100) there are two examples of this arabesque done as a *grand jeté* or big jump.

Third Arabesque   Both arms reach forward in a combination of the first and *second arabesque* positions. With no arm behind to visually counterbalance the upper part of the body, this position gives a feeling of reaching forward, of searching. To dancers, every momentary position that the body passes through requires the same attention, but to the spectator, certain beautiful shapes, like the arabesque, stay longer in the memory than others, particularly when seen as a final pose on *pointe* after a dazzling solo.

Notice how different this *third arabesque* looks from the romantic version on p. 48.

Arabesque Penchée In this *arabesque* the whole body leans forward, its different outline accentuated by the raised leg. Giselle the tragic heroine has taken her own life. Now she appears as a ghostly apparition before her former lover Albrecht. As she *penchées*, she gently crosses her arms before her in a gesture symbolising death and resignation.

The hips must be kept square as she leans forward, but the long romantic tutu will make any slight error less obvious!

The second example of an *arabesque penchée* is in the *first arabesque* position. The photograph shows the entire *corps de ballet* in the same position in LA BAYADERE, which was one of Marius Petipa's most successful ballets

56

in Russia at the end of the 19th century.

LA BAYADERE Act 3 is also famous for the incredibly dramatic effect when 32 members of the corps de ballet enter in a series of high *arabesques fondues* coming down a long incline. The corps de ballet both here and in SWAN LAKE are often asked to stand on one leg for long periods of time as a sort of backdrop to the soloists. This can become excruciatingly painful, and to make matters worse, they will then be expected to spring into action, even though cramp may have set in. If you ever watch a performance of either of these ballets from the wings, don't be surprised by any muffled mutterings coming from the dancers!

Arabesque Fondue   *Fondu* comes from the French word meaning to melt, or to sink down. A fondu is made by bending the supporting leg. Its soft, yielding and expressive shape can be seen in a number of different contexts. Firstly it is seen at the beginning and end of many big jumps like the

cabriole, brisé volé, grand jeté en tournant and the double *saut de basque*; secondly, because the fondu is a *plié* on one leg it can act as a take-off position between a step and a jump, or between two jumps. In SWAN LAKE for example it is seen as a series of little hops or jumps, and is used as a choreographic motif

by Odette, the Prince, and the Swans at
different times.

In this photograph from Act I of SWAN
LAKE Anthony Dowell shows just how much
feeling can be expressed by perfect line in a
fondu. The bend at the knee lowers the whole
body, and concentrates the eye even more on
the long line of the *arabesque*. At the same
time, there is no feeling of a static pose. The
great sculptor Auguste Rodin, who said that
for sculpture to have life it must give 'the
illusion of movement in progress', would
surely have been inspired by Dowell as he was
by Nijinsky.

The Attitude After the *arabesque*, the second most frequently seen shape in the repertoire of ballet positions is probably the *attitude*. In the inset from THE SLEEPING BEAUTY and on the left we see the *attitude croisée derrière* (or attitude crossed behind). The *attitude effacée derrière* (opened up, behind) on the right looks a little ungainly on the flat foot but on *pointe* it changes completely and can be a stunningly beautiful pose.

The attitude gives a feeling of enclosing space because of the wrapped-around quality of the raised leg which is bent at the knee (in front or behind) and is quite different from

the arabesque's long, harmonious extended line. It is this sculptural quality that makes the attitude so interesting in turns where it presents a constantly changing silhouette.

Like the arabesque it has its own special beauty and is also used in jumps, lifts, *promenades* and *pirouettes*. It is often seen as a midway position in slow unfolding movements, and in the *pas de deux* section there are two examples of this where the ballerina balances briefly on pointe in attitude, and then, thrillingly, opens out into an arabesque (pp. 129, 140).

Attitude Croisée Devant   Both the
drawing and the large and small photographs
show the *attitude croisée devant* on pointe. The
dancer on the right is rehearsing a sparkling
solo from THE SLEEPING BEAUTY, which
finishes with the leg crossed in front. Here
and in the inset photograph above, the
position of her arms and head, even her
expression seems to be saying: 'What did you
think of that?' Needless to say, this is usually

followed by an enthusiastic response from the audience!

In another moment from the Rose Adagio on the left, the taut backward curve of the upper body, the subtle alignment of head and shoulders and the asymmetrical position of the arms counterpointing the raised *working leg*, make a complex and satisfying sculptural shape.

Attitude Effacée Derrière   These
two pictures show variations of the *attitude
effacée derrière*, this time from behind and on
pointe. They show how expressive the back can
be in an *attitude*.

On the left, a lovely curved line runs from
her raised foot, along her leg and back, past
her upraised face and beyond. On the right

the same line leads us more directly to the
face, which is turned towards us.

Both of these attitudes are extremely
difficult to hold. Maintaining the height of
the leg, coupled with the slight rotation of the
upper back, requires strength, balance and
control. The spectator seldom realises what is
necessary to create such a lyrical effect.

64

Pointe Work　　The image of a dancer standing on *pointe*, is a universal symbol of ballet and is seen in no other form of dance. By increasing the dancer's height and the length of her legs, it lengthens the classical and romantic line. It was first used by Marie Taglioni in LA SYLPHIDE to give the impression of a sylph skimming along the ground. There is also a strong, steely quality hidden underneath its soft romanticism that can be used for dramatic effect.

Pointe work should never be attempted by dancers under the age of 12 because it puts tremendous pressure and strain on the feet and can easily distort them when the bones are not yet fully grown. For rehearsals and for pointe work later in the class, dancers take off the battered and softened pointed shoes they have been wearing, and change into harder ones. Even though every dancer has shoes

especially made by hand to fit her feet, brand new ones will first be banged on the floor or trampled on, to soften them up a bit.

In the drawing, the dancers are standing on pointe in three of the *basic positions*. On the left in the background, one girl stands with her feet flat on the ground, while the other leans on the *barre* testing her shoes. Both are in the *second position*. In the foreground, another dancer standing next to her *pas de deux* partner flexes her feet in a *turned-in* position here done as an exercise, but not often seen on stage. Behind her a dancer stands in the streamlined *fifth position* on pointe, which we will see in *bourrées* in the following pages, and *chaîné* turns (p. 82). The photograph from George Balanchine's APOLLO is a fine example of the *fourth position* on pointe.

Bourrées: 1   During the *adage* section of
class, dancers practise *arabesques*, *attitudes* and
other positions, slowly transforming the
body's outline from one position to another
in different *alignments*. As class progresses,
different types of movement are added,
turning them into steps, jumps or turns.
Bourrées are an exciting transformation of the
fifth position on *pointe*, a way of gliding
smoothly across or around the stage. The feet
make hundreds of tiny steps which give a
brilliant shimmering appearance to the legs.

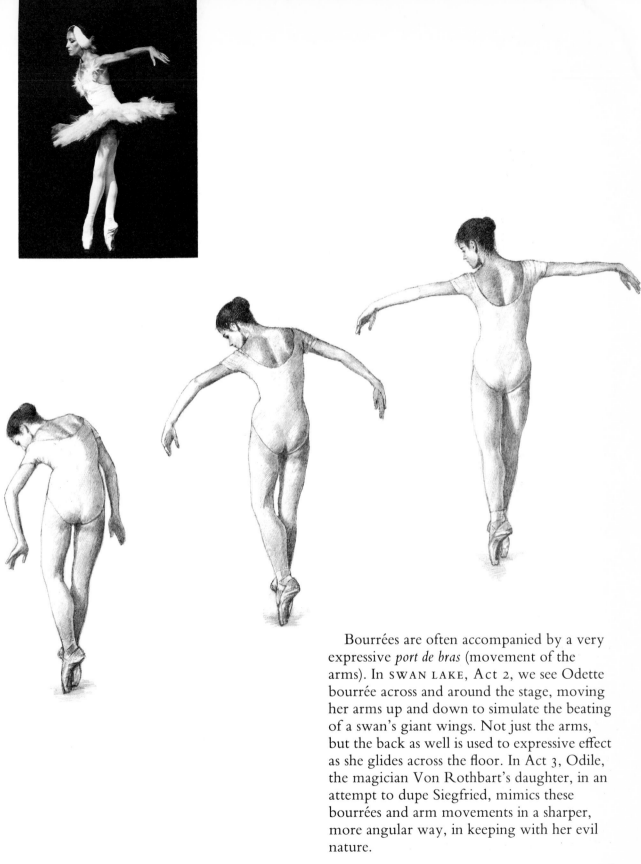

Bourrées are often accompanied by a very expressive *port de bras* (movement of the arms). In SWAN LAKE, Act 2, we see Odette bourrée across and around the stage, moving her arms up and down to simulate the beating of a swan's giant wings. Not just the arms, but the back as well is used to expressive effect as she glides across the floor. In Act 3, Odile, the magician Von Rothbart's daughter, in an attempt to dupe Siegfried, mimics these bourrées and arm movements in a sharper, more angular way, in keeping with her evil nature.

69

Bourrées: 2   Bourrées are done on the spot as well as moving across the stage, and here the shimmering of the legs may be even more obvious. In these drawings, we see part of a turn of the body, combined with another expressive *port de bras* which comes from the famous Rose Adagio in THE SLEEPING BEAUTY, act I.

Great artists and ballerinas understand how the arms and back should be used. It is not just a question of waving the arms up and down, slowly or quickly. Arms and back should be able to show a range of emotions from light-heartedness to sorrow. This will come more naturally to a dancer with an expressive and intuitive nature, and slender, mobile and graceful arms.

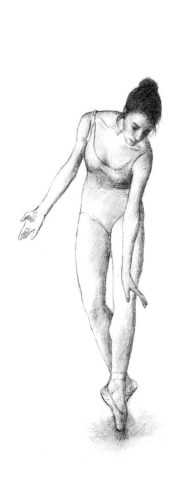

4

The Pirouette   One of the most exciting endings to a solo is a series of effortless *pirouettes*. Because there is always an element of risk involved, even the most experienced dancers worry about pirouettes and practise them every day in class. They make an impressive display when they come off perfectly, but off-balance pirouettes are impossible to hide.

Some dancers are fortunate enough to have a natural ability to balance and turn well. For them, as well as for dancers who do not mind falling over occasionally, pirouettes can be fun.

In the three rows of dancers on the left-hand page, you can see part of the *preparation* for a pirouette on *demi-pointe* from the *fourth*

position. First, they *tendu* to *second position* [1], then they bring the *working foot* behind and *demi-plié* in *fourth position* [2]. Pushing away from the floor, they turn swiftly into the pirouette with a whipping action of the head, while pulling the *working leg* up into the *retiré* position [3, 4].

Provided the body is perfectly balanced, and turns as a single unit after this initial push-off, the dancer gets enough momentum to keep the body turning a number of times simply by whipping the head around. This is known as '*spotting*', because the dancer focuses on one spot in the room or a small light at the back of the auditorium as long as possible before whipping the head back to the same spot again.

73

1

Pirouette on Pointe   The preparation for a *pirouette* on *pointe* is exactly the same as the preparation for the pirouette on *demi-pointe* on the previous page, except that here, she rises quickly on to full pointe [1] at the moment of push-off from a *demi-plié* in *fourth position*. In these drawings, we imagine that she has already made a number of turns and

is making her last complete turn before returning to fourth position with her arms extended forward in a firm and open position called *demi-bras*.

While turning, the dancer concentrates on a number of different things all at the same time. She must hold her stomach in, keeping her *working leg* well *turned-out* while the

74

muscles in the *supporting leg* must be well *pulled up*. She must maintain the position of the arms, and make sure that her foot does not slip out from its position next to the knee and overcross it. She must keep the body taut, but not too rigid while she turns. All this helps her maintain the imaginary axis running from the top of her head, through her spine, leg

and toe and into the ground.

Spotting, and turning in rhythm with the music keeps the pirouette going and helps the dancer know when and where to stop. The finish, when it comes, must be as strong, clear and decisive as the turn itself, especially as the dancer may feel slightly dizzy and must avoid any tendency to wobble.

1

Pirouette in Attitude   Although
pirouettes in *retiré* (with one toe drawn up to
the knee) can be done from almost any
position, *pirouettes* in *attitude* and in *arabesque*
usually start from the firm, wide platform of
the *fourth position* with the back leg
straightened out. This ensures that the body
will be correctly balanced over the supporting

leg, ready for the turn.

In the four drawings above, the dancer has
already pushed off, and is turning on *pointe*
with her arms raised in *fifth position*. In the
second drawing she passes through an *attitude
croisée derrière*. In the third drawing another
three-quarter turn takes her to *attitude effacée
derrière*, and she finishes in attitude croisée

derrière again. As the dancer turns, you can see the sculptural qualities of the attitude at every stage.

Pirouettes in different positions, like the attitude and the arabesque, give the *choreographer* plenty of choice when creating groups of steps. The finishing position, standing on the flat of one foot, is much more

difficult than the fourth position finish of the earlier pirouette. Tremendous co-ordination and balance are needed to arch the back and the attitude leg towards each other. The position of the open arms, apart from its pleasing shape, also acts as a counterbalance.

I

Pirouette in Arabesque: I In the following four pages we see two *pirouettes* in *arabesque* chosen to show how a very different emotional quality can be achieved by using different positions of the arms and legs. This

slowly turning pirouette is often used in *adage* sequences.

In the first drawing, the arms start in *second position*. As the dancer slowly makes two complete turns, they move upwards to the

fifth position. Raising the arms in the fifth position lengthens the long curved arabesque line, and forms a moving frame for the head. Turning in arabesque, with the foot so far from the centre of balance, is very difficult, especially when the arms move during the turn. Any loss of balance will tend to bring the leg down and spoil the expressive line of the body.

Pirouette in Arabesque: 2   The
higher leg in this *pirouette* gives it a more
brilliant image, an impression of technical skill
more than of emotion. Like the earlier turn
it is done quite slowly, but the higher leg gives

the feeling of sailing around a centre point. It
needs tremendous strength to hold the hips
completely square and level (see the first
drawing on the far right) while holding the

1

working leg out at right angles to the body. Even the best dancers will tend to displace their hips slightly due to the effort of turning with the leg in this position. Even if the dancer watches herself in the mirror, she may be turning too fast to see what is going wrong. The teacher will notice though, and will come over and correct her.

14   13   12   11   10   9   8   7

Enchaînement of Piqué and Chaîné Turns

Very often, towards the end of a solo, you will see the ballerina do a long series of very fast turns around or across the stage, accelerating to a dramatic finishing pose, or a leap off into the wings. The sequence will be made up of a linked series of turning steps of different sorts; hence the term *enchaînement*. (Enchaînements are in fact any group of linked steps or jumps.) In this example, starting from the right and moving to the left, we see *piqué turns* first, which look like a series of quick *pirouettes* with a step forward between each one. They are followed by *chaîné turns* where the dancer glides across the floor turning very quickly in *fifth position* on *pointe*, finishing in a firm *dégagé derrière* [14]. The effect is stunning, and there is a great deal that goes by too fast for the eye to register.

1 Piqué turns   She starts by extending her right foot forward [1]; *fondus*, swinging her leg round to the side and opening her arms out [2]. Then, she steps directly on to pointe and drawing her leg up into *retiré* [3] and bringing both arms inwards, she does a quick three-quarters turn [4]. Then she steps out sharply, on to pointe again and continues

82

[5, 6, 7] into another turn. In between each turn she must go from one leg to the other with a quick *coupé* (change of feet). Piqué turns can be done with double or even treble pirouettes, or with alternating single and double pirouettes. They can also be done in *attitude* instead of retiré, and then of course, the arms make an appropriate shape for this position.

2 Chaîné turns
From the last piqué she steps into a series of very fast turns on pointe [8, 9–12]. Chaînés are in fact tiny half-turns done alternately on one toe and then on the other. No other part of the body moves except the head, whipping around and 'spotting' with each turn. So the whole body must turn as a taut unit, perfectly 'placed', 'pulled up', and with the legs turned out. At the end of this whirling rush across the stage, she must be able to stop with a flourish, poised, and on balance.

Her partner will answer with an exciting series of jumps and turns around the stage. If they are performing the Black Swan *pas de deux* from SWAN LAKE the excitement will build even further with the turns that follow.

Fouetté Rond de Jambe en Tournant

After the Black Swan *pas de deux* Siegfried and the Black Swan (Odile) do alternating *variations* consisting of steps, jumps, and turns across and around the stage. There then follows a very long series of turns, hers being the famous *32 fouettés*.

These turns are a real feat of endurance, because by now, her *working leg* will be very tired. To get her momentum going, she goes into a double *pirouette* [1, 2], *fondus*, thrusting her working leg forward [3]; then, rising on to *pointe*, and opening her arms out forcefully,

1   2

3   4   5

she whips her leg sideways [4] and into another pirouette [5]. The rhythm of fondu-pirouette, fondu-pirouette continues [6, 7, 8] another 31 times; the push-off from the fondu giving a renewed thrust to each turn. The working leg must be kept at exactly the right height [4] so that the thigh does not need to move when the lower leg bends into *retiré* during the turn [5], in what is in effect a *rond de jambe* (see p. 31) going into a turn.

Nowhere is *spotting* more important than in fouettés. Any dizziness leading to a wobble could start her moving across the stage, and spoil the effect.

In the past, the 32 fouettés were always a virtuoso step. Now, with ever rising standards, any professional dancer should have the strength and technique to do them. But because the audience and ballet enthusiasts take them perhaps too seriously, dancers sometimes have a phobia about fouettés. It would be a shame for a ballerina who has given a wonderful performance to feel a sense of failure because her fouettés haven't quite come off and she has finished with a series of *chaîné* and *piqué* turns instead.

6   7   8

1

Tours à la Seconde

Immediately after Odile's *fouettés*, in SWAN LAKE Act 3, Siegfried comes on to do his *tours à la seconde*. The audience's excitement mounts with this equally dazzling display. He spins round, leg outstretched, at least 16 times, with a *plié* between each turn. If he's really confident, he will throw in a double turn after every fourth plié and finish with three or four *pirouettes* and a *lunge* to the knee [7].

He needs tremendous strength to hold his *working leg* horizontal with a straight back and perfect balance. For all turns, and particularly for a long series such as this, the *preparation* is vital. Here he *dégagés* to *second position* [1], *pliés* [2], then starts the turn by

2   3   4

pushing up on to *demi-pointe* on the *supporting leg* and thrusting the working leg up into second position [3]. These two movements coupled with the forceful opening out of the right arm, and the whipping round of the head, spin the body into the first turn [3, 4]. To keep the momentum going, he pliés [5] and *relevés* [6] during each turn, gaining extra push-off from the floor.

As with the *fouetté rond de jambe*, *spotting* is very important, since with so many turns, it is easy to get dizzy. It helps the dancer stay on one spot, and the weight of his fast-moving head helps lead him round, though to the audience, it may look as if his raised leg is doing all the work.

5   6   7

Petit Allegro

Introduction   After practising *pirouettes* the dancers move on to the next important part of the class, called *petit allegro*, where they jump for the first time. The first jumps are quite small, taking off and landing on two feet. Typical is the *échappé* on the left-hand side of the page which is a jumped version of the *second position*. To perform the échappé, they *demi-plié* in the *fifth position*, échappé (escape) their legs to second position in the air, as in the drawing, and land on the ground with their feet apart still in second position. Then they make another jump that finishes back in the fifth position. It is very important for the dancers to concentrate on the upwards spring, pointing their feet downwards as they

jump, as slack feet spoil the thrusting line of the leg. Echappés are also done in the *fourth position*. In the drawings above the dancers are seen in the *retiré sauté*. We have already seen the *retiré* position in *pirouettes* and later on we will see it in a big turning jump, the *saut de Basque* (p. 116) and in smaller ones like the *pas de chat* (p. 90) and the *ballotté* (p. 94).

All these little jumps prepare the legs for bigger jumps and for *batterie*, or *beaten* jumps. There is *petite batterie* of which *entrechats* (p. 96) are an example, where the legs *beat* rapidly past each other in a small jump, and *grande batterie* including the *cabriole* (p. 110), where one leg beats against the other in a big jump.

Pas de Chat   The *pas de chat* (or step of the cat) involves more than one movement of the legs and travels a certain distance through the air. Its best known use is probably in the dance of the cats (Puss in Boots and the White Cat) in Act 3 of the THE SLEEPING BEAUTY. The drawings may give the impression that the pas de chat consists of a series of poses; in fact it is one light, fast and snappy movement, with one foot chasing after the other. It does not require great strength and is one of the first jumps that children learn to do, both because the action of leaping off one foot and chasing it with the other come naturally to them, and also because they find the idea of the cat appealing.

The pas de chat is seen in many different contexts; for example, in the dance of the four little swans from SWAN LAKE, and here in LA SYLPHIDE where we see the Scottish hero, James, perform this step in a kilt. Another jump, the *double retiré sauté*, where both legs are drawn up together, looks similar to the momentary mid-way position of the pas de chat.

Assemblé   In this jump the two feet are brought together or 'assembled' in the air before the dancer lands on the ground. It is done in all directions on stage either as a small or as a very large jump and is frequently done with legs beating together in the air before landing. It is never a truly virtuoso step unless done as a very big *beaten* jump. It can also be performed while turning in the air.

Its main use is as one of the most common

linking steps in a dance, as it is a convenient way of moving from a step which ends on one foot, to another which starts on two feet from a *demi-plié*. Dancers learn to do *assemblés* in class, jumping up and down on the spot.

The assemblé in the drawings is the kind more usually seen on stage, which travels a certain distance in the air. The forward lean of the dancer's body emphasizes the feeling of flight.

Ballotté   This is a lighthearted, springy step. The legs toss backwards and forwards, the body leaning forwards and backwards with each change of weight to counterbalance them. The *ballotté* is not attempted until the dancer is at an advanced level because it takes great strength in the spine and feet as well as good balance. Any jumping step needs *elevation* or the ability to get off the ground, but for *petit allegro* steps like the ballotté there is a special quality called *ballon*. Ballon literally means 'bounce' and is an easy bounding and rebounding from the stage like a rubber ball being bounced against the floor. It is essential for keeping the momentum going in any series of small jumps. In GISELLE we see first Giselle (see inset) and then Giselle and Albrecht do a long series of ballottés.

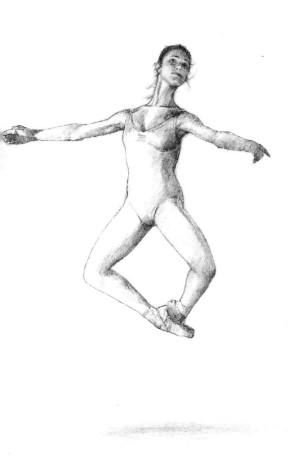

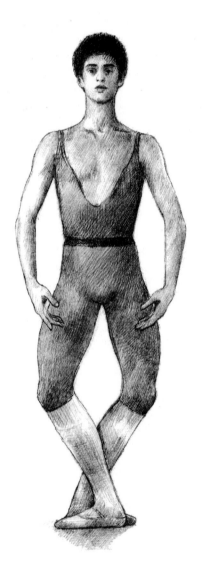

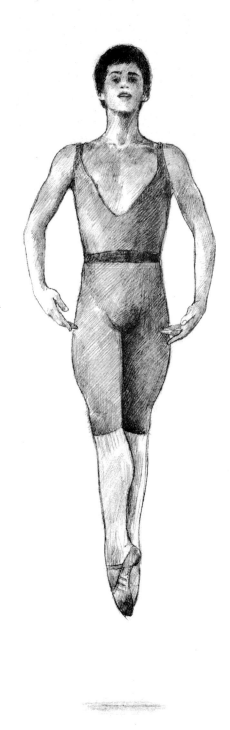

Entrechat   One of the most exciting steps in ballet is the *entrechat*, where dancers leap straight up in the air and beat their feet together in front and behind a number of times before landing. The whole leg crosses and recrosses – not just the lower half. The example shown here is one of the simplest as the feet have changed position only twice between take-off and landing. This is called an *entrechat quatre*. In *grand allegro* the dancers will do *entrechats six* where the feet cross over three times.

Done in a series, entrechats have a virile brilliant quality although they are done by girls as well as men. They are often combined with other steps and jumps. Serge Lifar, a dancer who began his career with Diaghilev's Ballets Russes, maintained that sparkling beats are easier to achieve if the dancer is slightly bow-legged, since his feet do not have to travel so far to cross and uncross.

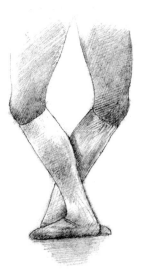

Grand Allegro

Introduction The climax of the class is *grand allegro*. The dancers are fully warmed up and ready to practise steps of virtuosity: spectacular leaps, turns in the air, and high *beaten* steps. To stimulate their interest, and test them to the full, the ballet master arranges *enchaînements* (chains of steps) that resemble parts of the finished ballet they will perform

later on the stage.

Classical ballet demands that men in particular should be able to perform steps of *grand élévation* with apparent ease, as they will need these movements for solo *variations*. Although girls do many of the same steps and jumps, in a high jump like the *grand jeté* in *attitude* seen above, boys tend to concentrate

98

on the height of the jump while girls emphasize extension of the legs. In order to have enough room when practising travelling steps, dancers go across the classroom from corner to corner in small groups.

By the end of class, the calm, unhurried pace of those first *pliés* has been replaced by an atmosphere similar to a Turkish bath. On stage that night, there will be no hint of effort or strain, but now the great crashing noise of eight simultaneous landings from a high jump may be followed by muffled curses, as one of the dancers limps away. The next few pages show a selection of grand allegro jumps.

Grand Jeté in Second Arabesque

Jeté is the name for any jump taking off from one leg and landing on the other, and the *grand jeté* is one of the highest, and for the spectator, one of the most exciting jumps in classical ballet. It should be smooth and effortless, seeming to defy the laws of gravity.

To produce this effect, the dancer should appear to soar through the air and land as lightly as possible. To do this requires years of training incorporating the sort of exercise we have seen throughout the class. *Turn-out* and complete control of the body's shape in the air must be maintained at all times.

Here are two extended versions of the *second arabesque* position. The crossed line of the legs and body, as the dancer on the left jumps diagonally towards us, gives a bright exuberant feeling. On the right we see the same jump done with the legs in *effacé* rather than the *croisé alignment* and the feeling is quite different. The slight curve of the upper back adds to the effect of the more continuous curve running from her arabesque toe to her upstretched hand.

Grand jetés like most other big jumps need a short run-up before take-off and the *glissade* on p. 104 is the one most commonly used.

Entrechat Six de Volé

This is an *entrechat six* executed during a large forward *assemblé*. The body arches slightly forwards from the waist as the fully stretched legs beat to the front below.

From a preparatory step or jump, the right leg is thrust sideways during take-off from a *demi-plié* in *fifth position*, followed swiftly by the left leg. The right leg beats in front [1] and behind [2], then comes in front again for the landing in fifth position. The right arm is raised in the direction of travel.

The *entrechat six de volé* is seen to great effect during male variations, in conjunction with other big jumps and turns.

Grand Jeté in Third Arabesque

The *grand jeté in third arabesque* combines the high arm of the *first arabesque* with the lower front arm of the *second arabesque*. Different shapes of the body and the qualities of movement and emotion that they suggest are an important part of the *choreographer's* vocabulary. Many other shapes are possible as well, of which *jetés* with the arms raised in fifth position (see *flick jeté*) and first arabesque are perhaps the most common.

In attempting to define the action of the legs in a grand jeté, one could say that both legs open out into simultaneous *grands battements*.

Flick Jeté and Glissade   The *flick jeté* is an exciting and explosive leap that derives its name from the action of the front leg in the jump. The dancer takes off with her front leg bent, and at the height of the *jeté* flicks it straight out in front. It is most often performed by women and usually matches a musical climax, or provides an airborne exit from the stage. In GISELLE Act 2 the ballerina performs a final diagonal series of flick jetés in one of her *variations*.

This jeté is typical of the new classical style. It is part of a trend towards more athleticism and gymnastic ability without sacrificing the expressiveness of the older tradition.

A jump like this needs attack, and a lot of flexibility in the back. The more compact lift-off with the front leg moving through *retiré* into this jeté equivalent of a *développé* allows the dancer's body to achieve more extreme shapes and a feeling of abandon. In the flick jeté illustrated here, extending the front leg

Glissade

104

downwards means that the back leg, as it moves up to form a straight line in the 'splits' seems higher than it really is. The legs are in fact in the same relationship as in the previous jetés, only their angle has been tilted downwards and the upper body thrown backwards at the same time. Flick jetés are also done in the same positions as ordinary *grands jetés*. The drawings on the left show a *glissade*, a common preparation for big jumps.

1   2

Sissonne   The *sissonne* is named after the scissor-like opening and closing movement of the legs during the jump. It is also the name given to all jumps that take off from two legs and land again on one. The *sissonne fermée* and the *sissonne ouverte* are done in all directions,

and while turning in the air as well.

In the sissonne fermée illustrated here, the dancer *pliés* in *fifth position* [1] and leaps backwards with his *working leg* raised at 90 degrees in the air in *effacée devant* [2]. On landing, he slides the working leg through

106

3

4

tendu [3], back into fifth position [4].

In the sissonne ouverte, the dancer jumps and lands in *fondu* with his working leg still extended in the position it assumed in the air.

In sissonnes, the working leg always extends away from the direction of travel. Here, in a backwards jump, it extends to the front. In a jump to the front therefore, the working leg would be raised behind in an *attitude derrière* or an *arabesque*. They can be done as big jumps because of the potential for a powerful take-off from a *plié* in fifth position.

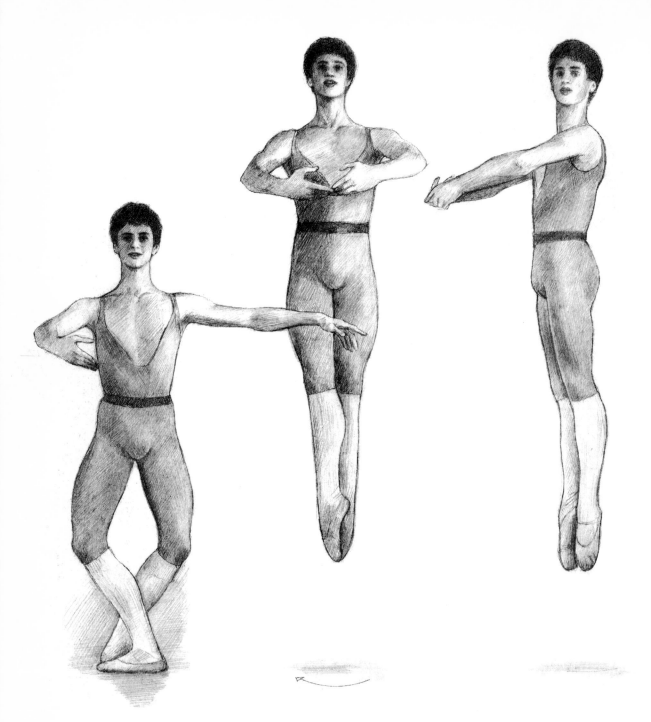

Tour en L'Air   In this spectacular jump, the dancer leaps directly upwards and turns one, two or three times before landing. It is seen very frequently as part of a chain of steps, or as the final flourish in a solo.

In the example here, we show only one turn for simplicity. Starting from a *demi-plié* in *fifth position*, the dancer springs from the floor, turning rapidly with the body absolutely firm and straight. If there is a wobble on landing the whole effect is spoilt. At some point while turning in the air, the dancer changes feet.

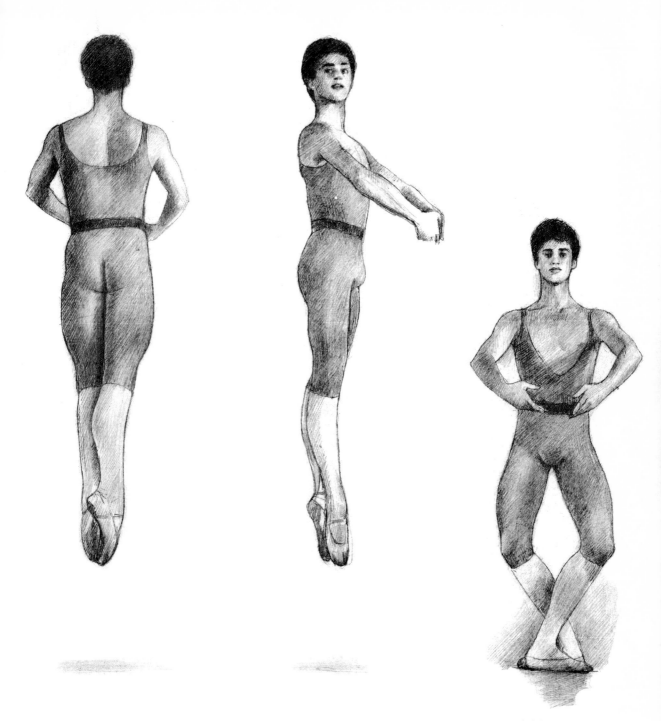

When he does this is entirely up to him, but as a result, he always lands with his feet crossed the other way round.

When done as the climax to a *variation*, the *tour en l'air* often finishes dramatically with a lunge to one knee (see p. 87) or the dancer may *relevé* from the finishing *plié*, into an elegant fifth position with his arms raised above his head.

Cabriole Derrière   The *cabriole* is very common in classical ballet and is impressive and exciting when done as a big jump. The dancer jumps, beats his legs together in front (*cabriole devant*) or behind (*cabriole derrière*) before landing.

In the drawings we see a cabriole derrière. In preparation for this jump, he will do a *glissade* (see p. 104), *fondu* in first arabesque [1] and take off, bringing the fondu leg up [2], to beat against the *arabesque* leg [3], before landing in a fondu in first arabesque again [4].

The photograph from Sir Frederick Ashton's THE TWO PIGEONS shows a splendid cabriole derrière. A long curving line runs down from the upraised hand to the feet, which are slightly blurred as they beat behind.

1

2

3

4

1 ⟶

Brisé Volé   This virtuoso step requires considerable strength and *ballon* and is best known from the Bluebird variation of THE SLEEPING BEAUTY, where the Bluebird does a series of them diagonally across the stage. The *brisé* is a travelling jump, forwards or backwards, with a *beat*. The brisés volés in the Bluebird variation alternate both types of brisé with a bird-like *port de bras*, and this, combined with the forward and backward swaying of the body and the beating of the feet, gives an impression of flight.

For the *brisé volé* to be effective, the spectator must see sparkling and clearly defined beats of the whole leg, with both legs fully stretched. Arching the body well forward, and then well backwards, with soft landings and springy rebounds in between is vital. The momentum must be kept going as any jarring of the step will spoil it, and bring the dancer to a halt.

Temps de Poisson   In Act 3 of THE
SLEEPING BEAUTY the Bluebird shows
Princess Florine how to fly, and with all his
bird-like jumps and turns, he hardly seems to
touch the ground. One of his most graceful
leaps is called, confusingly, the *temps de poisson*
(leap of the fish), whose curved shape we will
see again in the *fish dive* (p. 138).

   He does a series of these jumps along each
diagonal of the stage, interspersed with other
larger and smaller steps and jumps, like the
entrechat six de volé, the *chassé* and the *assemblé*.

   At first she answers his breathtaking
airborne *enchaînements* with rather awkward,
decidedly earthbound movements, till finally,
she soars off stage with him in a dazzling *flick
jeté.*

   Though the temps de poisson can be done
as a leap straight upwards from a *demi-plié* in
fifth position, to get height and a feeling of
suspension in the air, it is usually preceded by
an *assemblé.*

   The Bluebird Variation is one of the
supreme tests of a male dancer. It requires
great technical skill, artistry, *elevation,* and a
feeling of effortless ease. Teachers will always
stress the importance of a taut arched curve of
the whole body avoiding any bend of the
knees.

1   2   3

Double Saut de Basque   This spectacular travelling jump is often seen as part of a series of other big turns around the stage, notably in LE CORSAIR. It consists of a double turn in the air with one leg drawn up in *retiré* [3] and the arms *en avant* (in front) as here, or *en haut* (above). In another version, first one and then the other leg comes up into

4　　　　　　　　　　　　5　　　　　　　　　　　　6

retiré, like a giant turning *pas de chat*.

From a preparatory movement, the dancer steps out on to his left foot [1], *fondus* (not shown) *swishing* his right leg up into *second position* as he takes off [2]; then, bringing his left leg smartly up into retiré, and his arms en avant [3], he does two full turns in the air before landing in fondu [6].

Coupé Jeté en Tournant   There are many jumps for male dancers that go around the stage. One of the most common of these is the *coupé jeté en tournant*, also known as the barrel turn. It looks like a spiralling chain of *grands jetés* in *attitude* [1, 2, 3].

Each curving jump is followed by a quick turn on the ground which incorporates the landing of the previous jump, and the take-off for the next jump, together with a quick change of feet (the *coupé* a, b), which the spectator is unlikely to be able to see. These turns are extremely exciting to watch, especially if the dancer has good *élévation*.

1

The barrel turn is not difficult physically, but requires various 'tricks of the trade', which some dancers never master. Most important of these is leaning inwards on the turns. This counteracts the tendency of the body to fly off to one side instead of carrying on around. Many Russian dancers including Nureyev, seen in full flight in LE CORSAIR in the photograph, lean over so far that they are almost parallel with the floor.

The turning rhythm has a syncopated feel to it; the dancer seeming to spend twice as long in the air as in turning on the ground between jumps.

2: Rehearsal and Pas de Deux

Pas de Deux

Introduction   At the end of the class the dancers will be exhausted, and after thanking their teachers by clapping enthusiastically, there will usually be a break for refreshment before the day's rehearsals begin. The company may well rehearse several different ballets on the same day because the next programme must be started while the current one is kept up to scratch. So some time during the day, *pas de deux* will be rehearsed. There will also be rehearsals for the *corps de ballet*, and *ensemble* calls for the whole company.

Ballet enthusiasts are so used to seeing the male dancer as a brilliant solo artist, that they tend to underestimate the importance of his role as a partner in the classical and romantic pas de deux. This is partly because it is his job

to concentrate the audience's attention on the ballerina while he extends the limits of all her solo steps; helps her float effortlessly over impossible distances in the supported *grand jeté* and make innumerable turns in supported *pirouettes* and *finger fouettés*; and supports her in *promenades* and lifts.

In the pas de deux, the dancers must move as one body and must always seem to act under the same impulse. From the practical point of view, the ballerina needs a partner with whom she has an almost telepathic understanding and in whom she has complete trust. Otherwise her own dancing will be affected by a slight holding back, resulting from an unconscious fear of injury.

All movement is a joint effort; a high lift would often be impossible without her

discreet *plié* and push-off, added to her partner's effort. The pas de deux is a small drama at the heart of most ballets, and whether it is romantic, sad, lighthearted or aggressive, each dancer must contribute his or her share to their joint effort or risk at best a lifeless performance, and at worst a broken nose!

The photograph shows Anthony Dowell and Antoinette Sibley in Sir Frederick Ashton's production of CINDERELLA. He supports her in a variation of *third arabesque*. She could not possibly stand in this position by herself, since her centre of balance is thrown in front of her feet. The forward reach of the arms gives a feeling of yearning and the complementary shapes of their bodies adds to this impression.

Pas de Deux

In the photograph on the left, we see another moment from CINDERELLA. This time the ballerina stands on *pointe* and her partner gives her the barest possible support. As she leans lightly against his chest, he echoes the shape of her body with his own.

Many *grands pas de deux* represent moments from a love story, and the hero strives to demonstrate his passion for his partner, while at the same time showing off her beauty to best advantage to the audience. Sooner or later, some small gesture of hers will reassure

him that his feelings are reciprocated. In this instance it is the very act of leaning against him, symbolizing trust and tenderness.

The second photograph comes from the bedroom *pas de deux* in Sir Kenneth MacMillan's production of ROMEO AND JULIET to Sergei Prokofiev's haunting music. Here they dance joyfully during their brief wedding night. Unusual shapes of the body highlight tragic and ecstatic moments of this doomed love affair. The lighter mood of Cinderella is expressed through a more purely classical style.

Supported Attitude and Supported Arabesque

The drawing on the left shows a supported *attitude croisée derrière* and the drawing on the right shows a supported *first arabesque*. At its simplest, the support of the partner enables the ballerina to stand longer on *pointe* than she would normally be able to unaided. As a development from these two positions, her partner can walk around

her, turning her on pointe in a slow supported *pirouette* in *attitude* or in *arabesque*. This is known as a *promenade*.

The attitude on the left is also often seen as the finishing position of a series of supported pirouettes, see p. 131. The boy must be very careful to keep all his steps at the same distance from his partner's foot, otherwise he will easily overbalance her.

Promenade in Attitude   A famous example of the *promenade* in *attitude* comes in the Rose Adagio from THE SLEEPING BEAUTY. Four princely suitors promenade Aurora in turn, each supporting her with his outstretched hand. Between each promenade she raises her other arm and balances on *pointe*. This *fifth position* of the arms is sometimes known as '*en couronne*' (like a crown), which is very appropriate in this context. At the end, she again raises her arm, balances, then as the music swells to a crescendo, opens out her

arms and attitude leg into a stunning *arabesque effacée* as seen in the last drawing.

The spectator may not realise that this is extremely difficult. When she is supported at the waist (previous page) a *promenade* is relatively easy, but here the only physical contact is between their two hands.

Eye contact is reassuring to both of them and helps him avoid throwing her off balance; but the secret of this promenade lies in the tension of the 'S' shape made by their arms bracing against each other as they turn.

Supported Pirouette

The girl's preparation in this type of *supported pirouette* is exactly the same as for the unsupported pirouette. Her partner stands directly behind her, with his hands lightly supporting her at the waist. With this support she may do more turns than she normally could unaided, because if she does get slightly off balance, he can correct her imperceptibly. The dancers must have a very close understanding, because an unsympathetic partner could easily ruin a perfectly good series of pirouettes by being heavy-handed.

In this type of pirouette she finishes in *attitude croisée derrière* on *pointe*, and her partner is ready to support her at the waist opening out one arm to *second position* to match hers, when she has finished turning. (See inset.) In other types of pirouette where she starts on pointe (instead of from *fourth position*) her partner will start her turning by feeding her waist through his hands.

Finger Fouettés   In the supported *pirouette*, the dancer is able to push away from the floor but in the *finger fouetté,* she starts on *pointe* and the impetus for the turn comes mainly from pushing off from her partner's lower hand, and from the whipping round action of her raised leg. She starts by bringing her right leg up into *retiré* [1], then she *développés* to the front [2] and whips her leg to the side and back into retiré again as she turns [3, 4], lightly holding his middle finger directly above her head. With his support, she can turn many times like this.

A very famous use of finger fouettés occurs in SWAN LAKE Act 2. Odette does one finger fouetté supported by Siegfried. He then *promenades* her while she does a little trembling movement with her working leg *sur le cou de pied* (*petits battements serrés battus*). This is followed by two fouettés and another promenade, then three fouettés, and finally four.

1

2

3

4

Supported 'Fall' In this supported fall from the White Swan *pas de deux* Siegfried lowers Odette so that she faces us. Her weight does not, in fact, rest on his thigh as it seems to in the pictures, so she needs to jam her back foot into the floor to stop herself from sliding away to the right. She holds herself in a gently curving *fifth position* against his outstretched arm, the shape of his body harmonising with hers.

Her partner must place his hand in exactly the right place not just to support her correctly, but also to avoid causing her excruciating pain by catching her under the rib cage.

Swallow Lift   This is one of the most difficult lifts and can be terrifying for the girl, because she naturally feels that if she tips forward, she will land on her head. More important than strength in the success of such a lift is the co-ordination between the partners. She must hold herself absolutely still and balanced in her swallow-like pose, while he turns slowly round. To do this he must have positioned his hands in just the right place on her hip bones. These are fairly visible on a slim dancer, and the teacher may explain to young students that this is exactly what they were designed for!

Présage Lift   The *présage* lift – named after the ballet LES PRESAGES – is one of the highest in ballet, and is frequently seen in contemporary as well as classical dance. In order to get so high off the ground, it is vital for the girl to help her partner by pushing off [2, 3] with her lower leg just as he starts to lift her. Watching the présage lift from the auditorium, the spectator is probably unaware that what looks like a straightforward lift for the boy, is actually a supported jump from the girl's point of view. Like all jumps it starts with a *plié* or *fondu* [2].

1

2

This lift, though similar to the previous one, feels more secure because her partner's hands are further apart and she cannot topple forwards. If something does go wrong she can always put her foot down (in rehearsal at least). A common exercise for the partner to work on is to lift the girl straight up from an *arabesque*, without her doing a plié to help him. This would not be possible for a smallish man if his partner was too tall for him.

To make the best use of her plié in performance, he bends his knees, straightens and locks his arms under her while she jumps.

Then he can lift her the rest of the way by unbending his legs. It is, of course, far easier to lift a heavy weight with the legs than with the arms, and weightlifters use the same technique once they have 'snatched' the weights up to shoulder level.

Dancers who try to increase their lifting ability by weight training alone are missing the point. Co-ordination and technique are far more important than brute strength, and the smaller male dancer can easily lift someone his own weight or heavier if he has that technique.

3

4

Fish Dive   The *fish dive* is one of the most spectacular displays in classical ballet. In the classroom example shown here, the girl is lowered into the fish dive from a supported *first arabesque* with her partner taking her weight on his thigh and with her right leg hooked around his back. In performance, this thigh is often hidden by her *tutu*, adding a feeling of danger.

Fish dives can follow a number of steps and lifts. In the *Grand Pas de Deux* of THE SLEEPING BEAUTY we see Aurora fall twice into the fish dive, first, as in the photograph above, from a series of *pirouettes*; then, at the climax, she falls into a final fish dive straight out of a high lift. Both dancers then turn to the audience, arms outstretched to receive their applause.

THE SLEEPING BEAUTY I: Two of the
great classical ballets that every young dancer
or ballet-goer is likely to see are THE SLEEPING
BEAUTY and SWAN LAKE. We have already
seen a number of examples from solos and *pas
de deux* from these two ballets. The examples
shown here and in the following pages have
been chosen to show the special quality of
slow supported *adage* movements.

Aurora, who never bowed to anyone
before, sinks down in homage to her prince.
She is very vulnerable, as he raises her up on
to *pointe*, and supports her while she brings
her leg up through the *retiré* position into
attitude. He shows his admiration and love by
the noble and dramatic way that he raises her,
and then, when she is perfectly balanced, steps
back leaving her proudly alone on pointe in a
stunning *arabesque*.

THE SLEEPING BEAUTY 2: This is a wedding *pas de deux*; the atmosphere is happy and intimate. The *choreography* is noble and restrained at the beginning, building up to the more flamboyant high lifts and *fish dives* later on. As the Prince supports Princess Aurora with one hand, she *développés* her leg towards him and he raises his other arm to echo her *port de bras*. She leans back as far as possible, then suddenly whips (*fouettés*) her body round, finishing in a triumphant supported *attitude croiseé derrière*.

This fouetté requires even greater co-ordination between the dancers than any spectacular lift. It is a real feat of balance. Not only must she be well 'placed' and perfectly on balance as she turns, but he must judge to perfection the moment when he releases her hand, and transfers his support to her waist.

It is like a speeded-up version of the *fouetté* of *adage* on p. 32.

SWAN LAKE I: In the White Swan *pas de deux*, Prince Siegfried is captivated by Odette, Queen of the Swans. She has already explained with the use of *mime* (see pp. 154–5) that she has been enchanted by an evil magician, and must remain half-swan, half-human until she is released from the spell by someone promising to love and marry her. All her movements are sad, graceful and regal; he moves around her, trying to reassure her and

demonstrate his love.

In the first four drawings, she slowly unfolds her leg (*développé*) and inclines with a swan-like gesture of the raised arm towards him, then yields, falling back almost as if she has given up hope. He steps towards her, catches her around the waist, and gently lowers her in the direction of her fall, while all the time protecting and supporting her.

continues

Tchaikovsky's sad cello solo gives an air of tragic intensity to their movements as Odette's wings surrender and brush, almost lifelessly, against the ground. But as Prince Siegfried raises her gently upwards, his love, and the knowledge that it will break the spell, seems to give her new hope. Her arms and leg rise gently into *arabesque*, and she relaxes for a moment into an *arabesque fondue*.

Different parnerships will bring their own interpretation to this special *pas de deux*.

Later in SWAN LAKE these same *adage* movements are mimicked and even at times caricatured by Odile, the magician Von Rothbart's evil daughter. Both characters are, of course, danced by the same ballerina, giving her the greatest opportunity in classical ballet to demonstrate artistry and expressiveness.

SWAN LAKE 2: In the Black Swan *pas de deux* Odile flirts with Prince Siegfried, who believes her to be his beloved Odette. The wicked Odile tries to get him to betray Odette by asking her to marry him. Here she leaps

teasingly away in a *grand jeté en tournant*
ending in an *arabesque*, which she follows by
sinking, in mock submission, to the ground
in a swan-like pose.

Finally class and rehearsal are ended, and the dancers have had at least two hours to rest. Now they are half way through the evening performance. The curtain is about to rise on the second act of SWAN LAKE. The murmur of the audience has died down, the house lights dim, and the orchestra begins to play. Dancers check each others' costumes and headdresses; fasten hooks and eyes, and adjust *pointe* shoes. The stage manager issues instructions to the stage hands through their headsets as they check the scenery. The working lights dim and smoke begins to pour on to the set. At the last moment the dancers hurry off stage to take up their positions in the wings, and the curtain rises on a deserted and misty lakeside scene.

I am   the *queen*   of the *swans*.

bad man turned me into a swan   *but*   if a man promises to *love me*

Appendix

SWAN LAKE: Mime   Mime is a sign language that is often used in the older ballets where the complicated plot cannot be conveyed by dance alone. Simple naturalistic gestures, a hand over the heart for 'I love you', are easy to understand and have the same meaning in many different cultures. Other gestures which would have been understood by any theatre-goer 100 years ago now need explaining to a modern audience.

I see over there   a lake *of my mother's tears.*   *One*

and *marry* me   and *swears* to love me forever,   I shall be a swan *no more.*

Here is a well-known mime passage from SWAN LAKE, Act 2, which uses many of the more common gestures and is still retained in many modern productions. Princess Odette is telling Prince Siegfried that she and her companions have been put under an evil spell by the magician, Von Rothbart, who has changed them all into swans. Only if a man promises to marry Odette and love her forever will the spell be broken.

Index Glossary

note: numbers in *italics* indicate illustrations

Adage from the Italian word adagio meaning 'at ease'. Describes slow graceful, flowing movements with beauty of line, balance and control; *adage* section of class *39*, 68, 78, and *38–87*; similar supported movements in *pas de deux 128–147*; see also *arabesque*, *attitude*, *battement fondu*, *battements tendus*, *développés*, *pirouettes* and *pliés*

AFTERNOON OF A FAUN *14*

Albrecht 56

Allegro a brisk or lively movement; *petit allegro 88–97* includes smaller jumps like *entrechats* and *assemblés*; *grand allegro 98–118* includes larger jumps like the *cabriole*, the *grand jeté* and turns in the air

Alignments the direction the dancers face on stage, governing the shape and angle of the body seen by the audience; Introduction *40–41*; *croisé* to *effacé 42–43*; *effacé* to *croisé 44–45*; *écarté 46–47*; 42, 68, *101*

APOLLO 67

Arabesque one of the most important positions of the body in ballet. The dancer balances on one foot with the other leg extended behind, and with the arms extended to make a variety of harmonious shapes. The terms first, second and third arabesque are named after different positions of the arms; characterised by its long elegant line *42, 45, 50–51*, 60, 61, *76, 77, 107, 137, 149*; *first, second* and *third arabesque 51*; *supported arabesque*

in the classical, romantic and modern styles *48–49*; *first arabesque 52–53*, 103: on *demi-pointe 50*; on *pointe 51*; *jeté* in *103*; promenade in *53, 127*; supported *126, 138*; *second arabesque 54*, 103: *grand jeté* in *100–101*; *third arabesque 55*: *grand jeté* in, *103*; supported *48, 123*; *pirouette* in *arabesque 78–79, 80–81, 127*; *arabesque effacée 128, 129*; *arabesque fondue* (with a bend of the *supporting leg*) *33, 57, 58–59*, 100, *147*; *arabesque à terre 42*; *arabesque penchée 56–57*

Ashton, Sir Frederick THE TWO PIGEONS 110; CINDERELLA *122*; ROMEO AND JULIET *152–153*

Assemblé a jump from one foot and landing on two, with the feet coming together or 'assembling' in the air *92–93, 102*, 115

Attitude an important position of the body where the dancer balances on one leg with the other leg lifted in front (*devant*) or behind (*derrière*) with the knee bent at right angles. One arm is held in a curve above the head, and the other arm is extended to the side. Different *attitudes* are named according to the position of the body (*alignment*) in relation to the audience *60–61*, 68, *140*; derrière *107*; devant *34*; *attitude croisée devant* (crossed in front) 42, *62–63*; *attitude croisée derrière* (crossed behind) 45, *61, 76*; supported *126, 130, 131, 143*; *attitude effacée derrière* (open, facing behind) 42, *61, 64–65, 76*; on *pointe 64*; *attitude effacée devant* (open, facing to the front) *45*; *grand jeté* in *attitude 98, 118*;

pirouette in *attitude 76–77*, 127; and *piqué turns* 83; *promenade in attitude 127, 128–129*

Aurora *128, 138*, see THE SLEEPING BEAUTY

Avant, en forwards, towards the audience

Balanchine, George APOLLO 67, BALLET IMPERIAL 42

Ballon the quality of jumping with a light springy bound and rebound from the floor 95, 112

Balloté a light-hearted step, with the body tossing backwards and forwards on alternate legs 89, *94–95*

Barre one hand rests lightly on the barre during early exercises in class *24–37*, 24, 34, 36, 67; *barre-work* 38

Basic Positions all steps start from, go through, and finish in one of these positions of the feet. See *first, second, third, fourth* and *fifth* positions, and the positions of the arms that go with them *16–17*, 67

Battement literally a 'beating' movement of an extended leg along the ground or in the air. There are two types 1) *petit battements* like *battements tendus 28–29*, 35, 36, 42, 45, 73 where the leg and foot stretch away from the body with the toe on the ground; *battements glissés 30* where the toe slides out more forcefully, just leaving the ground; and *battements frappés* where the ball of the foot strikes

Variation a solo dance 96, 102, 104,
109; Bluebird variation 112, 115
see *pas de deux*, grand

Working leg the dancer stands on
the *supporting leg* while moving
the *working leg* 30, 32, 42, 45, 63,
74, 81, 84, 87, 106

Select Bibliography

Kay Ambrose *The Ballet-lover's Pocket-Book*, Adam & Charles Black, 1944
Mary Clark and Clement Crisp *The Ballet Goer's Guide*, Michael Joseph, 1981
Giambattista Dufort *Trattato del Ballo Nobile*, Felice Mosca, Napoli, 1728
Richard Glasstone *Better Ballet*, Kaye and Ward, 1977
Gail Grant *Technical Manual and Dictionary of Classical Ballet*, Dover Publications Inc., 1967
Sandra Noll Hammond *Ballet Beyond the Basics*, Mayfield Publishing Co., 1982
Lincoln Kirstein, Muriel Stuart, Carlus Dyer *The Classic Ballet*, Alfred A. Knopf, 1980
Serge Lifar *Lifar on Classical Ballet*, Allan Wingate, 1951
Jane Robbins *Classical Dance*, Holt, Rinehart and Winston, 1981
Nikolai Serrebrenikov and Joan Lawson *The Art of the Pas de Deux*, Dance Books Ltd, 1978
Leslie Spatt, Nicholas Dromgoole *Sibley and Dowell*, Collins, 1976
Agrippina Vaganova *Basic Principles of Classical Ballet*, Dover Publications Inc., 1969

A word of warning
Many steps illustrated in this book, including pointe work, lifts, and jumps can be dangerous if attempted by young or inexperienced dancers or by non-dancers. Ballet training at any level should always be supervised by a qualified teacher.